Let's Draw
The Nativity

Written by Anita Ganeri
Illustrated by Rachel Conner

Hi! I'm going to help you use this book. I'll give you drawing tips, and tell you where to find this story in the Bible!

STANDARD
PUBLISHING
Cincinnati, Ohio

GETTING STARTED

Have you always wished you could draw but never known where to begin? Then look no further! This is the book for you. In it, you can find out how to draw the story of the first Christmas when Jesus was born in Bethlehem.

Below are some of the things you may need to get started. Before you begin, let's make sure you have everything you need.

Look in the back of the book for your grid pages.

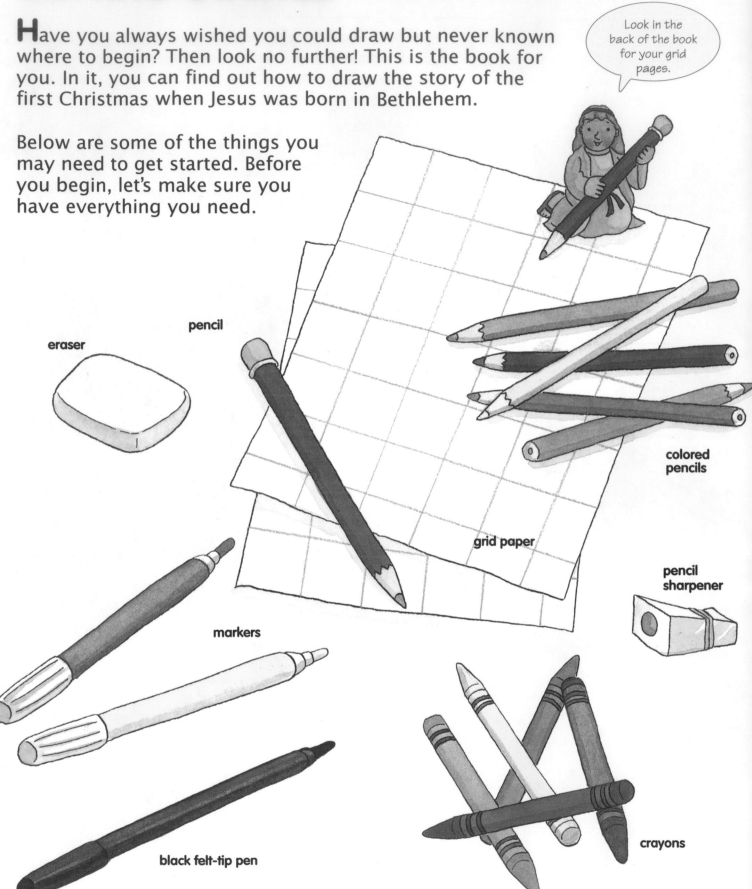

eraser

pencil

colored pencils

grid paper

pencil sharpener

markers

black felt-tip pen

crayons

USING THE GRIDS

At the back of this book, you'll find some grid pages. They'll help you to follow the drawing steps by showing you exactly where to add each new line. Pull them out carefully. If you run out of grids, ask a grown-up to help you photocopy or draw some more.

1 & **2** Copy each drawing, step by step, onto your grid paper noticing where the drawing should touch the lines on your grid. Draw lightly in pencil first. Each new step is shown in blue to show you exactly what to draw next.

3 When you have finished, go over the lines you want to keep in felt-tip pen and erase any leftover pencil lines.

Remember: what's new is blue!

4 Congratulations! Now you have a finished drawing! You can color your picture using your colored pencils or crayons. The final step of each drawing is shown in full color – so you can copy it. You'll also find some coloring tips on page 24.

MARY AND JOSEPH

You can read the story of Mary and Joseph in Luke 1:26-38 and 2:1-7.

Mary and her fiancé, Joseph, lived in the little town of Nazareth. One day, an angel came to visit Mary. He told her that she would have a baby boy, called Jesus. He would be God's son and he would be very special. He would grow up to save people from the wrong things they were doing and lead them to God.

Some time later, Mary and Joseph had to travel to Bethlehem. It was a long, tiring journey. But when they reached Bethlehem, they couldn't find a place to stay. Every room was full. Then a kindly innkeeper took pity on them. He let them stay in his stable. And it was there that baby Jesus was born.

Here are some details you can add to your pictures.

When you have learned to draw the characters and animals in this book, try drawing this scene of Mary and Joseph traveling to Bethlehem.

Manger

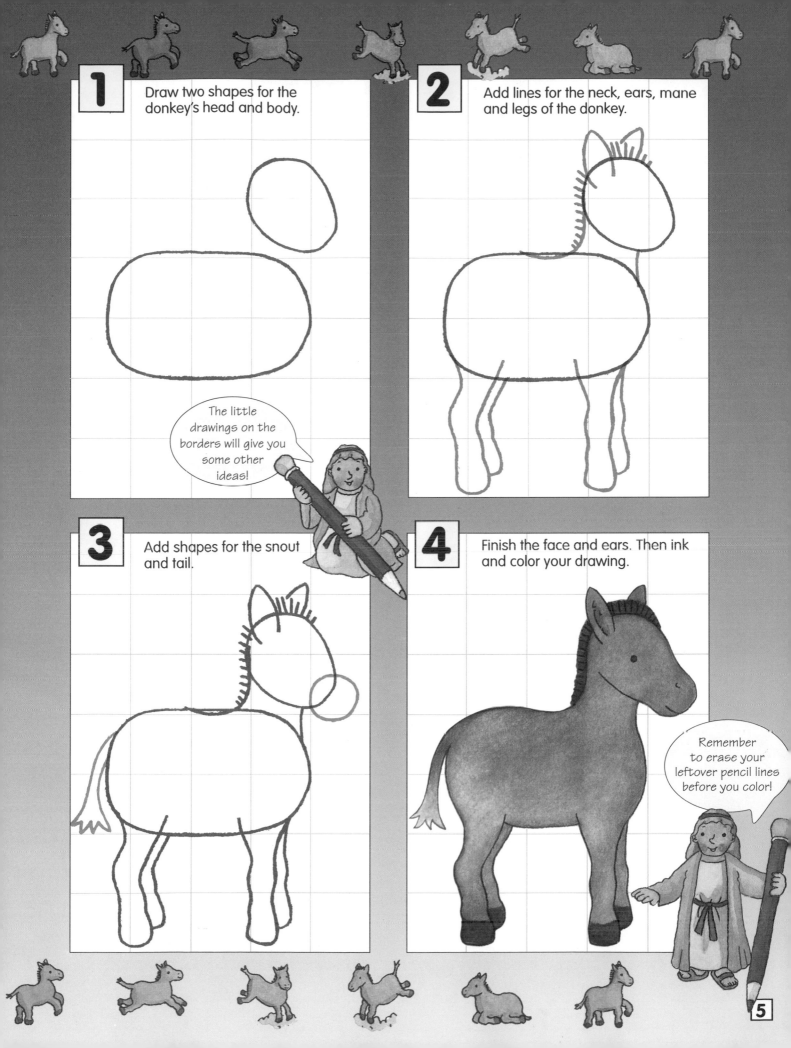

1 Draw two shapes for the donkey's head and body.

2 Add lines for the neck, ears, mane and legs of the donkey.

The little drawings on the borders will give you some other ideas!

3 Add shapes for the snout and tail.

4 Finish the face and ears. Then ink and color your drawing.

Remember to erase your leftover pencil lines before you color!

5

1 Draw three rounded shapes for Mary's head and body.

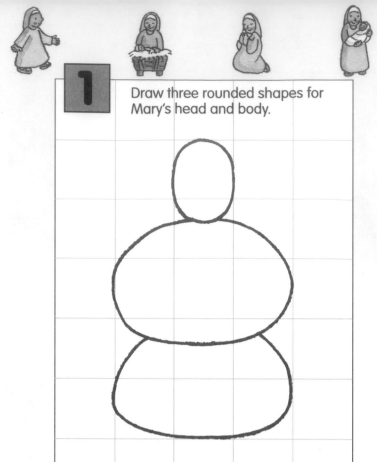

2 Draw the shapes for the baby. Use curved lines for Mary's veil.

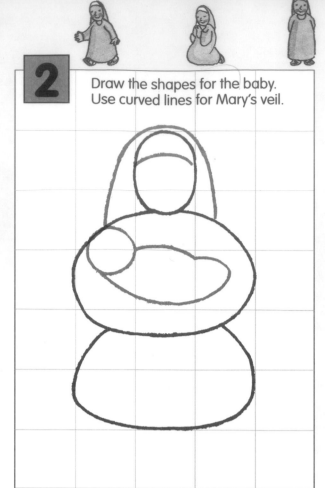

3 Add shapes for a foot and hands. Add lines to Mary's clothes and the baby's blanket.

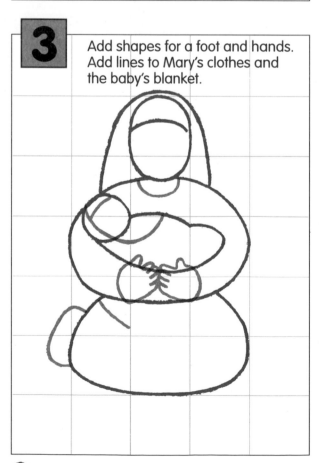

4 Finish both faces. Add more lines to the clothing, and draw a sandal and toes.

Then ink and color your drawing.

1
Draw the shapes for Joseph's head and body.

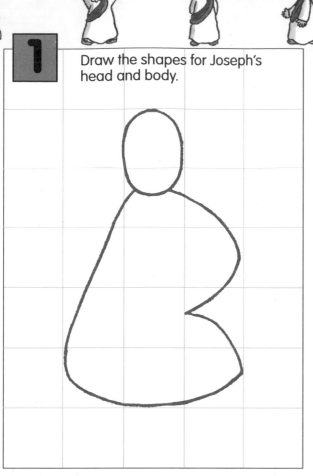

2
Add his arms and his hands.

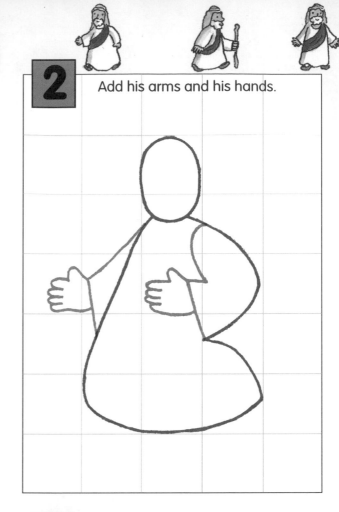

3
Add lines for his ear, feet, curly beard, sash and headdress.

4
Finish the face. Add toes and sandals, and more detail lines on the clothing.

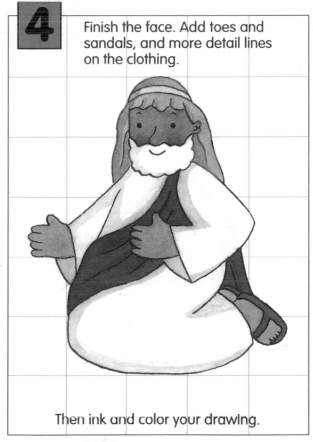

Then ink and color your drawing.

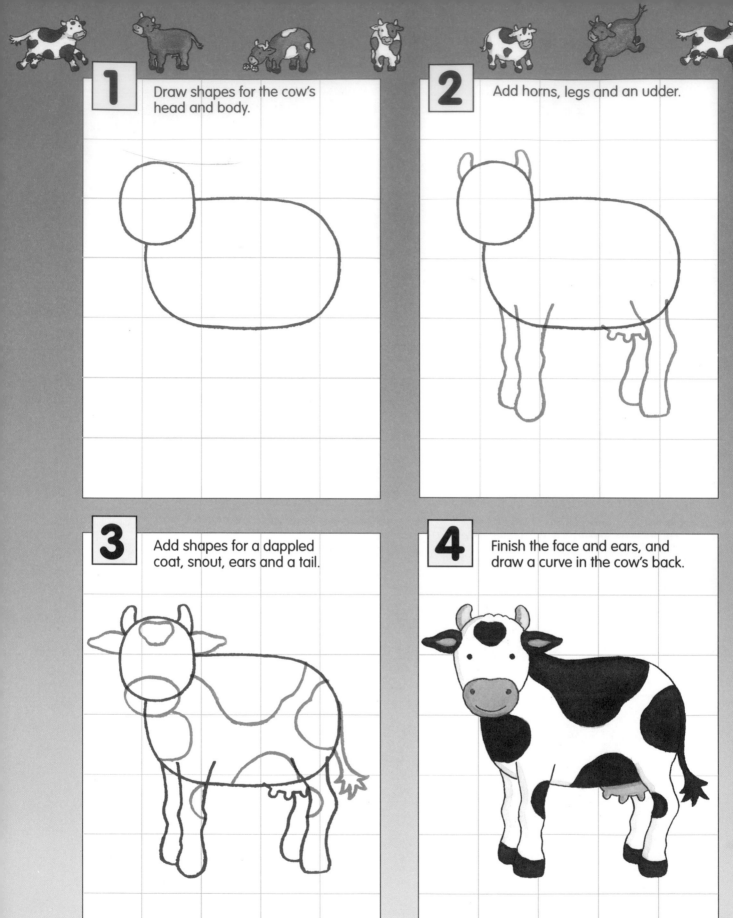

1
Draw shapes for the cow's head and body.

2
Add horns, legs and an udder.

3
Add shapes for a dappled coat, snout, ears and a tail.

4
Finish the face and ears, and draw a curve in the cow's back.

Then ink and color your drawing.

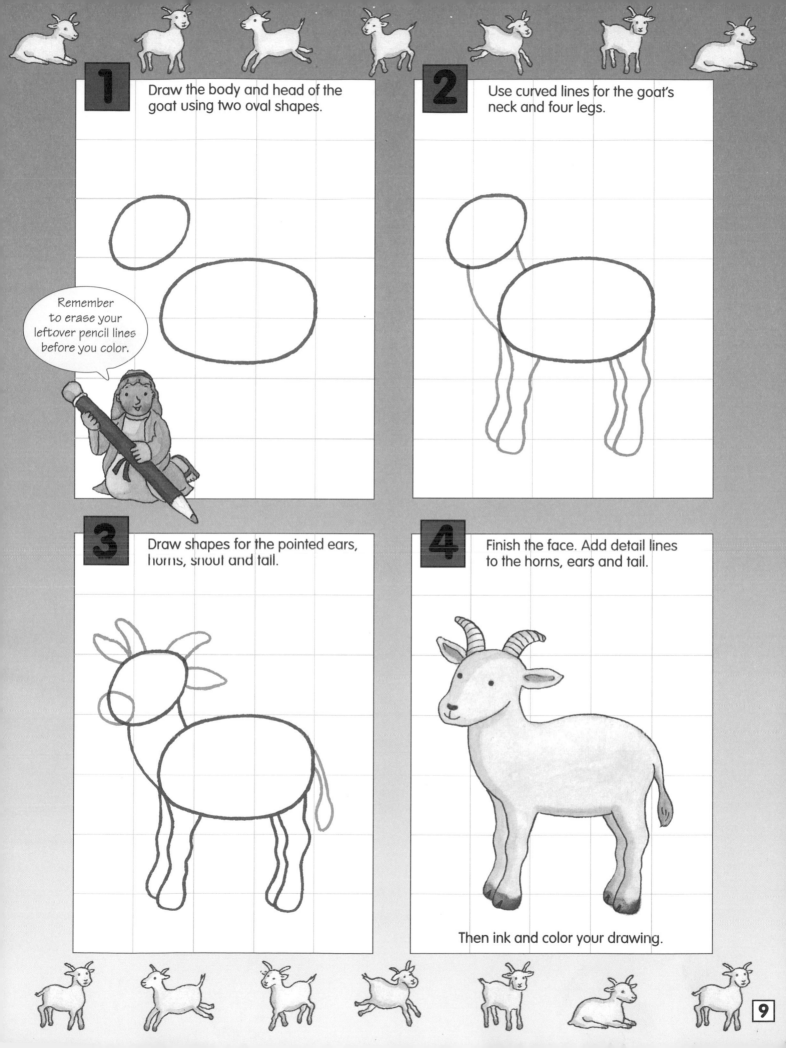

1 Draw the body and head of the goat using two oval shapes.

Remember to erase your leftover pencil lines before you color.

2 Use curved lines for the goat's neck and four legs.

3 Draw shapes for the pointed ears, horns, snout and tail.

4 Finish the face. Add detail lines to the horns, ears and tail.

Then ink and color your drawing.

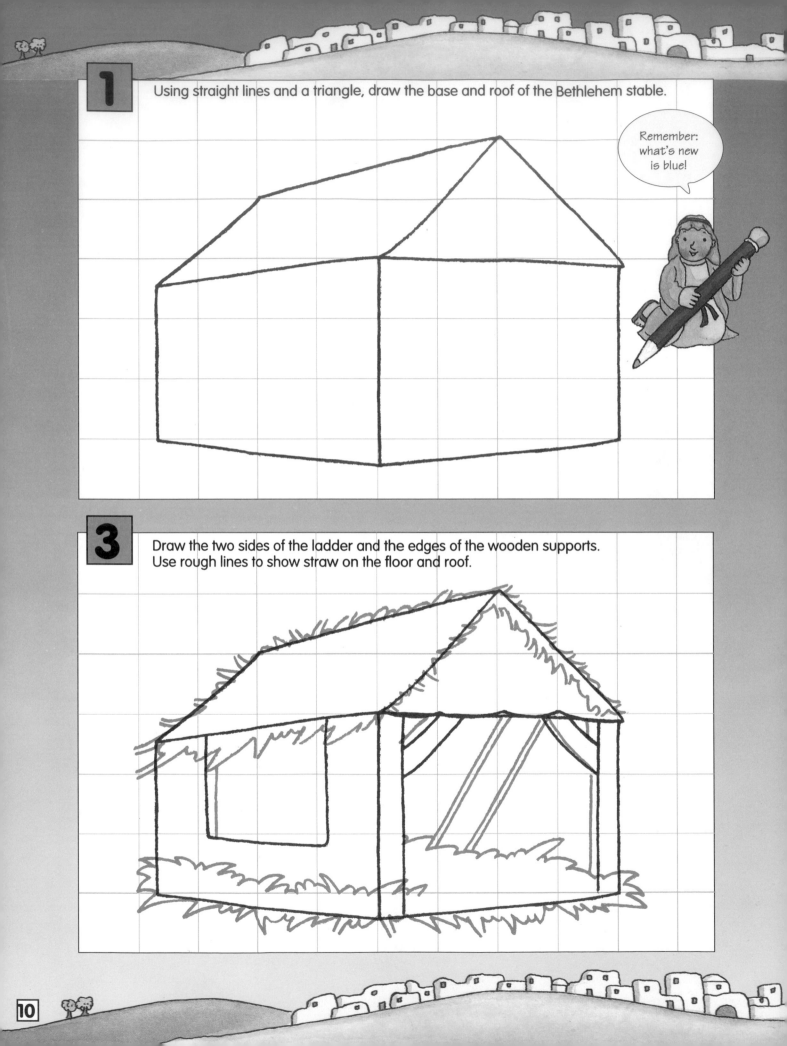

1 Using straight lines and a triangle, draw the base and roof of the Bethlehem stable.

Remember: what's new is blue!

3 Draw the two sides of the ladder and the edges of the wooden supports. Use rough lines to show straw on the floor and roof.

2 Draw wooden supports at the front, and a window in the side wall.

4 Add rungs to the ladder and lines for the wooden planks. Then ink and color your drawing.

Now you can add some of the animals you have learned how to draw.

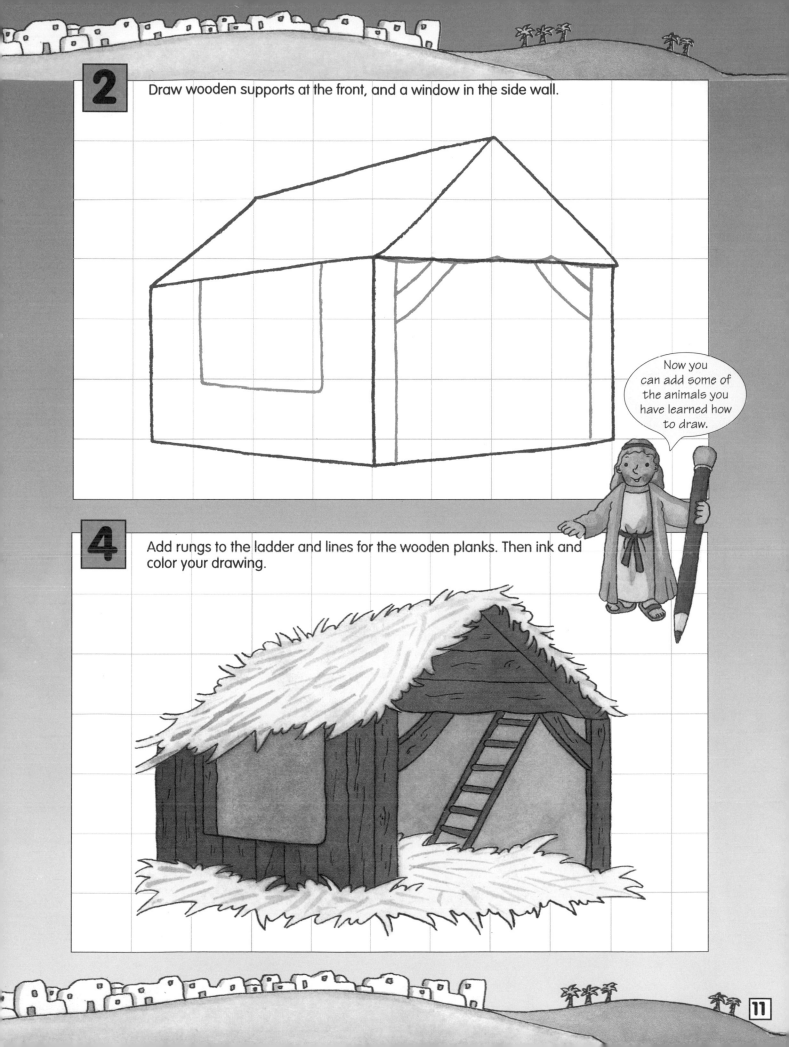

Grass and rocks

THE SHEPHERDS

You can read the story of the shepherds in Luke 2:8-20.

On a hill, just outside Bethlehem, some shepherds were watching over their flock of sheep. It was a quiet, still night and the shepherds were half asleep. Suddenly, the sky was filled with a bright, shining light and an angel appeared. The shepherds couldn't believe their eyes. But the angel told them not to be afraid, because he brought good news. And he told them about Jesus' birth in the little stable. Then the sky filled with angels singing, "Glory to God." When the angels left, the shepherds set off to find Jesus.

When you have learned to draw the characters and animals in this book, try drawing this scene of the angels and shepherds.

Here are some more details you can add to your pictures.

Tree

12

1 Draw an oval for the shepherd's head and a bell shape for his body.

2 Add shapes for the arms, feet and part of the scarf.

3 Add shapes for a headdress, hands, staff and sandals. Add more lines to the clothes.

4 Draw a belt, the tail of the scarf, and the shepherd's face. Then ink and color your drawing.

1 Draw the head and a curly, wooly body shape for the lamb.

2 Add four sausage shapes for the legs.

3 Draw shapes for wool and ears on the lamb's head. Add the tail.

4 Add the face and detail lines for the wool.

Then ink and color your drawing.

For more drawing ideas — look at the borders!

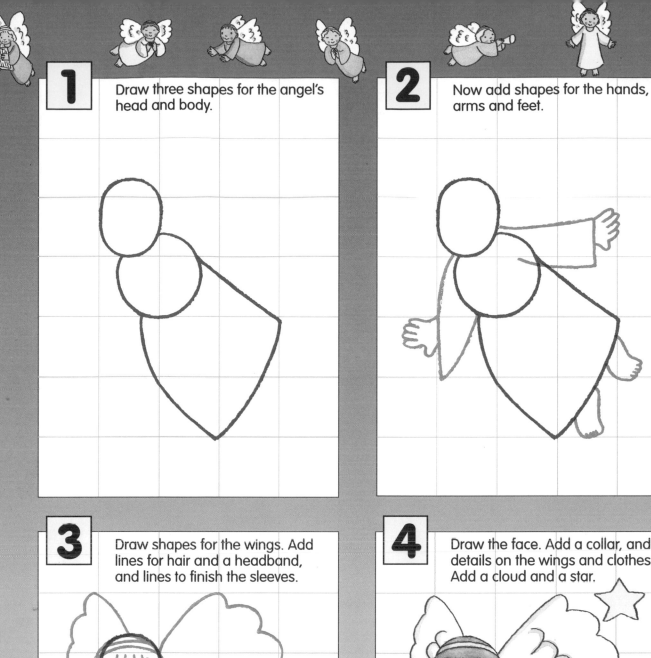

1
Draw three shapes for the angel's head and body.

2
Now add shapes for the hands, arms and feet.

3
Draw shapes for the wings. Add lines for hair and a headband, and lines to finish the sleeves.

4
Draw the face. Add a collar, and details on the wings and clothes. Add a cloud and a star.

Then ink and color your drawing.

ANIMALS IN ACTION

So far, you have drawn animals standing still. Now try making them move. To do this, you need to change the positions of their bodies and legs. You can see how to do this in the pictures shown here.

Remember to look back at the borders for even more action ideas!

Start with the lamb position you learned how to draw on page 14. Stretch out the legs and tail to make the lamb run and leap.

Start with the donkey position you learned how to draw on page 5. Raise the tail and stretch out the legs to make the donkey gallop.

PEOPLE IN ACTION

You can make people move, too. First, draw the people following the instructions on the step-by-step pages. Then draw them in different positions to make them look as if they are moving.

Remember to look back at the step-by-step drawings first.

Start with the shepherd position you learned how to draw on page 13. Stretch out the arms and turn the body and feet to make him walk. Turn the staff, too.

Start with the wise man position shown on page 19. Bend his legs under him and close his eyes to make him kneel and worship.

Treasure boxes

THREE WISE MEN

You can read about the three wise men in Matthew 2:1-12.

Far away, in the East, three wise men were riding along on their camels. They were following a great new star that shone brightly in the sky above them. The wise men knew the star was a sign that a new king had been born. And so they set off to find him. The star led them to young Jesus, their new king. They knelt in front of him and gave him precious gifts of gold, frankincense and myrrh.

When you have learned to draw the characters and animals in this book, try drawing this scene of the three wise men.

Here's how to draw two of the wise men's treasure boxes.

1 First draw shapes for the wise man's head and body.

2 Add shapes for an arm, a hand, feet and a headpiece.

3 Give the wise man a face, a beard and a treasure box to hold. Add a collar and other lines to his clothes.

4 Add another arm, toes and sandals, and details to the clothes. Decorate the treasure box. Then ink and color your drawing.

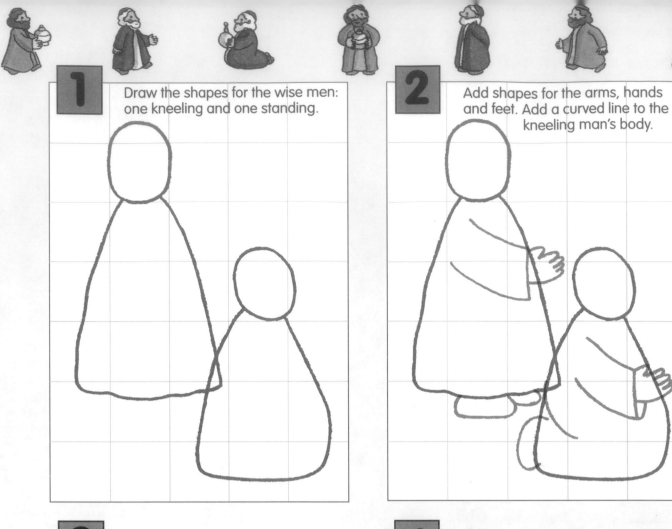

1
Draw the shapes for the wise men: one kneeling and one standing.

2
Add shapes for the arms, hands and feet. Add a curved line to the kneeling man's body.

3
Add shapes for hair and beards, ears, headpieces, clothes, sandals and treasure boxes.

4
Add faces and toes, and details to the clothes and treasure boxes. Then ink and color your drawing.

1 Draw a circle and an oval for the camel's head and body.

Remember: what's new is blue!

2 Add curved lines for the camel's neck, chest and four legs.

3 Draw shapes for a saddle, tail, ears and snout.

4 Finish the face and ears. Draw decorative lines on the saddle.

Then ink and color your drawing.

PUTTING IT ALL TOGETHER

Now you're ready to create your own nativity scene. Try putting together all the animals and people you've learned how to draw, then add a background. Here you can see just one way of creating the scene. But it's up to you – you're the artist! You can put the scene together any way you like.

Star

Tree

House

Use the following grid pages for your drawings. Don't forget to make photocopies!

23

COLORING YOUR DRAWINGS

When you've finished the outlines of each of your drawings, have fun coloring them. Here are some tips on ways to color.

You can try different color paper, too! Try rough paper or smooth paper for different textures!

Markers:
Use these to get a smooth, even finish. Also, by placing your marker at different angles, you can make thin or thick lines.

Colored Pencils:
These are good to use if you want the texture of the paper to show through.

Crayons:
You can blend different colors of crayons together to make a totally new color.

Try mixing different materials – you could color in pencil over an area you colored in marker, for example!

24